# A Quick Guide to Psychic Art

## By

## Saleire

Copyright ©Sarah Tracy 2013

# About the Author

Whilst going about my business, wondering what to do on my spiritual journey, I began painting to fill in the gaps between writing books, meditating, spiritual healing and creating spiritual pieces for healers. I still didn't know why I was painting portraits, as I couldn't really paint, which was frustrating to say the least, but I soon found out that Spirit had other ideas and psychic art was one of them. I realized that the portraits were just a way to help me learn how to draw and to give me a hint about where this would lead me. Spirit are there to guide you, but if you are not paying attention it might take a couple of hints before you get the message.

# Introduction

For those of you who are new to the world of psychic art, it's simple, Spirit have devised a way to show that they have survived by giving the gift of a portrait by someone who has no knowledge of what your family in Spirit look like. I think it is the best evidence you could possibly get from Spirit. They do not mind if you paint them, sculpt them, or in my case, draw them digitally, they don't mind which medium you use, as long as you are trying your best to get a likeness.

How does it work? Like any form of spiritual gift, Spirit draw close enough to touch your energy field, transferring their thoughts and images through your aura so that you can see, feel and hear them and all you have to do is be open.

If you want to become a psychic artist, you don't have to believe they will work with you, you just have to believe in yourself. Spirit will work with anyone who wants to help other people understand that there is survival after death and they will be by your side even if you just want to give it a try, but will arrive by the truckload if you are dedicated enough to stick with it. So don't worry about their part in it, just believe in yourself.

When Spirit guide you to do psychic art, whether you can draw, or not, is of no consequence to them, they know that with their help all things are possible. Which is just as well because I have no training in art school, or in drawing portraits and am completely baffled as to why they would want me to do this work, but I have learned that when Spirit inspire you to do something it's best to just go with the flow as it is always the right direction, even though you might not think so at first.

When I began doing this work I had hoped that they would come and sit still until I had finished, but it's a little bit more complicated than that. I am sure there are artists out there that have their guides sit in front of them but with my work, I get a glimpse of a cloak, or flowing hair, then bit by bit they guide me through the painting until it is finished. Half of the time I have no clue whether I am drawing a guide, male or female, a member of a family or a pet, as it comes in such a way that I am usually the last to know. I've come to see this as a good thing as it stops any influence from me.

My guides influence can be subtle and sometimes in your face, but there is always guidance when you want to work for Spirit. They don't mind if you can't draw or can't see Spirit, they will find a way to help you. Fortunately, I see Spirit and hear them, but this doesn't make it any easier as you have to be proficient at portraits to be able to just look at a face and draw it. So they use other ways to influence me with step by step images that help me to draw how they want it.

I am here to tell you that you do not have to be a great artist to work with Spirit, all you have to do is listen to their guidance. With each painting there will be a new challenge, how to draw a nose, getting the shading right, eyes and ears, I had no clue how to do these, but they are clever in their guidance, so clever in fact that I did not even know they were training me long before I tried to do psychic art.

It began with painting Phil Lynott, from the group, Thin Lizzy. For some reason he kept popping into my mind and so I started painting him, and just as soon as I was finished, I wanted to paint another portrait of him. I couldn't do it from memory, so I found some pictures of him and did my best.. I had always loved Phil and so painting him was a complete joy for me, even though it challenged me on every level to do so.

When I began painting, I could feel Phil drawing close and when I was finished he would smile and I would move on to the next one. But then another spirit drew close to me, one who is always here, due to my son's admiration for him. Christopher Wallace, 'Biggie', as he is known, wanted me to paint him and so I did and then others came. But I did not see this as psychic art (I'm not the brightest spark in the fire) I saw this as just painting, but then Nate Dogg came along and wanted a painting for his mother for Mother's Day. I did the painting and sent it to his mum and she accepted it and said it was one of the best she'd received, which made my day.

Spirit were becoming stronger and stronger each time I did a painting of someone that had died and I knew then that they were blending their spirit with the painting. When this happens, people can see the painting change, it can jump off the wall, smile, blink or even wink. I have seen this on many occasions. I could see lights at my side and once a full spirit body of light stood next to me, I figured that was Nate, as he had just passed over to the world of Spirit and I was working on his portrait.

I know now that they were training me to do portraits, but it still didn't hit me that they wanted to do psychic art, like I said, I am not the brightest spark in the fire.

I hope by showing you how they work with me it will give you the confidence to see that you can do psychic art if you want to, all you need is dedication.

## Table of Contents

Chapter One – The First Paintings

Chapter Two – Tarot, Faces, Hands and Feet!

Chapter Three – Children, Aliens and Hybrids!

Chapter Four – Go With The Flow

Chapter Five – Be Happy With New Challenges

Chapter Six – Family in Spirit

Chapter Seven - Step by Step

Chapter Eight – Messages

Chapter Nine - Drawing Your Guide

# Chapter One

## The First Paintings

### Phil Lynott 2011

Phil was one of my first paintings, I had no clue how to draw, not really and I'm still amazed when I look at this painting that it came out as well as it did. You would not believe how hard it was for me to figure out how to draw a hand, or the studs on his wristband and how to get his hair to shine, but somehow, as I began drawing, the brush just seemed to take control and it all worked out it out in the end. I began to hear, almost immediately, a voice saying, 'No, make it smoother' or 'Too dark' and so on, until it began to look remotely like a face. I also felt the colors just jump out at me, I am useless as combining the right colors for anything but somehow they just seemed to mix themselves and suddenly the right shade would appear out of the mush of paint on my palette.

Phil is a very strong spirit, I had seen him often around the house and was quite amazed at some of his antics. For instance, I used to listen to a radio show and each time they would play a song called, 'Sarah' by Thin

Lizzy, Phil would appear just before they played it and point to the radio, and every time he did this, the song Sarah came on. I was so amazed that I would have fun telling the DJ that the next song was Sarah a second before he played it and he would always write back, saying, 'How do you do that?' I would tell him it was Phil. Thankfully he was a very spiritual man and understood. I still think this was the most amazing evidence any spirit could have given me and I am eternally grateful to Phil for this wonderful gift.

Christopher Wallace 2011

Biggie was my next painting, I had seen him around the house and knew I should paint him. I am clairvoyant and often see Spirit, but not well enough to draw them, so I really didn't think of this as psychic art, but even then, there was guidance, 'Don't do the whole face' they repeated over and over and so I didn't. I knew Biggie liked this and I was happy with it too. It hangs in my son's room where we often see Biggie, eating chicken and relaxing.

Nate Dogg 2011

The day we heard about Nate Dogg dying we were so sad. I loved his voice and felt him so near that I had the urge to paint him too. I kept feeling that he wanted to do something for his mum for Mother's Day. As I was seeing a full spirit of light standing next to me, I decided it was the right thing to do and sent it to his mother as a tribute as I knew his Spirit was in the painting. His mother graciously accepted it as a gift and hopefully it hangs on her wall, as I am sure Nate would like that. I felt with this one that he will make things happen wherever this painting is and I'm sure things are happening right now in his mother's house. Maybe lights are turning on and off, or he may even smile, but I am sure he will come up with ways to let his mother know how much he loves her. It still amazes me how much they come through when they want to convey their love, whether it is guides, family members or pets, they all come through with such amazing feelings of love and it is a joy to feel their enthusiasm as I paint their portraits.

Marilyn 2011

If you have never painted hair, or ruby-red lips it is the hardest thing in the world, I nearly gave up a million times on this painting. They help you, but they don't do it for you. You just have to trust that it will turn out alright in the end and though it took me a long time, I was reasonably happy with the result. Marilyn was close and I could feel her spirit, but I still didn't think of this as psychic art, I always thought that they would just stand in front of you or, move your hand so it does the right stroke and not wobble all over the page hoping to hit the right spot with the paint. No, they don't do that, well, not yet anyway. I am on a journey and have not reached the destination yet, so who knows how it will have progressed by the time I have finished this book.

I did all the paintings in 2011. The urge to paint was so strong that I did one every day until I ran out of canvas and paints. I began to wonder what I could do with them. I had all these paintings in my room, but nowhere to send them. I decided that they had to go somewhere so I gave them to anyone who liked them. This gave me a lot of pleasure and I thought, that's it, I'll just paint and give them away as gifts. But in time, I was exhausted, painting every day, tired from trying to figure out the process and not earning a penny. I had to earn some money and I had to take a break from painting to see what spirit had in mind for my next project.

Phil 2011

Before I did this, there was one more painting to do and I was thrilled how it turned out, Phil again, and this one I knew had to go to his mother. I wasn't sure how it would be accepted, so I kept it for a while, but in 2013 a situation presented itself for someone to take it to her. Smiley Bolger, a friend of Phil, always puts on a show to celebrate Phil's life, called, 'The Vibe' and so I emailed him and asked him if he would like something to raffle at the show for their chosen charity. He wrote back saying he was delighted with the paintings and could I get them to Dublin in 24 hours. I managed to get this done off they went to their home in Dublin. They raffled off Phil with the guitar, Smiley kept the other and his mother chose this one for herself.

That was the end of that, I heard nothing more and was happy that Phil was home with his mum. Then, one night the phone rang and I heard, 'Can I speak to Sarah please, this is Philomena Lynott', I nearly had a heart attack, but she calmed me down and she told me how much she loved the painting and how I should come over and visit Dublin. She is a wonderful person and it is on my list to do this year, 2013, if it's the last thing I do. I never could figure out why Phil kept visiting me, but now I do. However, I still didn't really catch on that this was psychic art. I just figured that he liked this painting and wanted his mother to have it, but I didn't know he had a phone call up his sleeve. I have never been so thrilled to talk to someone in my life, she was so lovely and gracious, it made me want to grab the first plane to Dublin to have a cup of tea with her and visit Phil's grave.

I hadn't realized it but they were helping me work on mixing colors and drawing faces even then. I didn't understand that this was what they wanted me to do as they never force you to do anything. They just guide you, inspire you and give little hints here and there to let you know that you chose this work to do before you incarnated and they are just reminding you of this choice. It helps if you are open to their guidance, but sometimes things just happen and you can't figure out why you are doing it, but in the end it will all make sense.

Anyway, I decided that that was that with the portraits, they had all gone to their mothers, or their fans and I didn't think much more of it. I took a break from painting and asked spirit if there was anything else they wanted to do and I got a resounding, 'Yes!'

Sadly I cannot put these photos in this book as they are copyrighted by the artists who took the pictures, but you can see them on my site, which you will find at the end of this book if you wish.

## Chapter Two

## Tarot, Faces, Hands and Feet!

To my surprise they wanted to design Tarot cards, write some more books and some other bits and bobs. From the minute I began the cards I couldn't stop, the cards just flowed. First came 'Inner Realms' then 'Rainbow Tarot'. I wrote the books for them and within a few months had a publisher for both. I was thrilled to bits but figured that was that, until another Spirit came by to say hello, Pamela Colman Smith, who had another idea.

Pamela wanted her deck, the original Rider/Waite deck to be reproduced in all kinds of colors and completely made up of fractals. I decided

I would go along with it and set to work. To my amazement they began to fall together in no time and I loved working with them and felt that she had not felt truly involved in the making of the original deck, so she was delighted to have her say this time. We worked into the night and her spirit runs through all of them. If I got one particularly right I could feel her excitement. It was a wonderful time and I hope she has other plans for more cards, as she is a lovely, gentle spirit and a joy to be near.

My deck is called 'Stormrider' and are completely filled with fractals. It was hard to do these, each piece of clothing had to be made up of hundreds of fractals and once again, drawing hands and feet nearly drove me mad! And the faces, oh my God, I nearly threw them out so many times in frustration, but in the end, they came together and I know that she is pleased with them, as I am. They are full of her energy and so good for reading to say the least.

You might be asking what this has to do with psychic art, well, have a look at the cards and you will see all the shapes of bodies, faces, hands, feet, shoes, and so much more, even then they were teaching me how to draw and how to make a picture come alive with color.

They truly are a gift from Spirit to me and to all those who read the Tarot and I have the spirit of Pamela to thank for them.

In honor of Pamela, I tried to get a blue plaque put up in her name to show the world, where she used to live and to remind people of her artwork, but they decided that she wasn't famous enough! How on earth can they come to that conclusion? Everyone who loves tarot knows Pamela and I'm really sad that the blue plaque committee didn't say yes to putting one up in Battersea. One day, maybe I'll make my own plaque for her and sneak up in the night and put it on there to honor her memory.

Stormrider

By the time I finished this deck I was ready for something else and could not think of anything to do, but, as always, spirit have had another plan, guess what, another tarot deck! I was not amused. I thought it was time for a break, but then I kept looking at his particular tarot deck and couldn't resist.

Tarot of Gold

I loved the Visconti deck from the minute I saw it, marveling at the gold and the intricate work of the artist, and before I knew it, I was working on producing another deck of cards and to be honest I am quite pleased with my interpretation. Tarot of Gold is a shimmering deck of gold, and I am sure Spirit are happy with them.

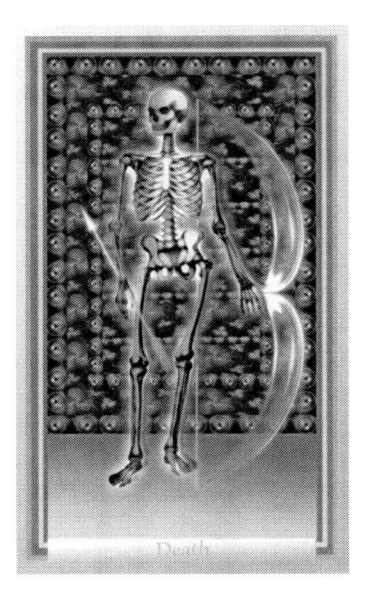

Mind you, it wasn't easy, not only did they want faces and hands in this deck, but horses too! I struggled with each and every hand, foot and face of these cards, each time changing the shape of the foot a hundred times, but I did love making these cards, they are full of color and just shimmer in gold. Hopefully the spirit who worked with me on these is as happy as I am with the result. I am sure he is glad to have a break too though. I began these in 2013 and when I was finished I thought, rats! Now I have to write a book for them! I was really tired so decided to leave that for later. I thought I was taking a rest from my spirit work, but they had another plan and not one I was expecting at all!

Chapter Three

Children, Aliens and Hybrids!

My lovely husband bought me a birthday present, a Bamboo drawing tablet. I looked at him and said, 'This is wonderful, but what on earth am I going to do with it? I can't draw!' I thought I would hardly ever use it and it would sit in the cupboard gathering dust, but now I couldn't be without it. No paint messing up the carpet, no water dripping onto my lap and if it goes wrong, you can just rub it out and start again without having to sand the canvas and scrape off the paint. It was a godsend, or should I say, spirit-send!

One day, while just doodling with it, I had the idea that maybe I could draw spirit. I wonder where that came from? I began drawing a little child who popped in to say hello, but from the very beginning I could only draw

German - Names: Hans and Grieber - Hazel Eyes
Freckles - 8-9 years old - Hoola-hoop - Fayre
Lost at Fayre

pictures as a child would and knew that I was completely wrong for the job. Me draw from scratch, never! What on earth was I thinking! Here are a couple of drawings of little children who came to see me, I just could not draw!

I felt so sorry for the children, I had done such a terrible job. As hard as I tried they kept coming out like this! Then it dawned on me, the artists in spirit who were helping me with these pictures were children! And so, of course they would draw like children! But I was still not convinced completely, so I asked for a drawing that someone would recognize, then I would know I was on the right track.

To my surprise, I went into Facebook and there was a request from a friend to draw her friend's daughter. I was thrilled, until I read the bit about her daughter being a hybrid child, extraterrestrial and human! Boy, when spirit ask to you work, they sure pick a hard one to get you going!

But, I had asked them, and they had sent this request, so I began to draw the little girl. As soon as I started drawing her I had the feeling that I had drawn her before, but it wasn't until I had finished it that I knew which one. Here is the first one that I did as human and the second one as a hybrid child. She had just wanted to show herself to her mother as both.

To be honest, I was sweating buckets giving this to her mother. I could feel her close and she definitely existed, but you just never know if you have gotten it right and this is a very sensitive subject, you have to get it right! I was dreading that she would disregard it as nonsense, but instead she accepted it and said that she had been shown by her daughter the very sign on her forehead. I was thrilled and so thankful to spirit for trusting me to get it right. The next three or four drawings I did were extraterrestrials. They came to say hello and tell me that they were my three guardians who watch over me. The first one was the matriarch, the comforter. The second, the Patriarch, the protector and the third was the messenger or communicator. Now the third one I had problems with, his facial designs were elaborate and I thought, really? Can someone like this exist? (I should know better!) I posted it on Facebook, biting my nails in case they all thought I was mad, but almost immediately one of my friends told me that they had seen the very same guy in their dreams! I just had to believe in what I was getting and not think I was going bonkers! They seemed like such lovely souls but totally unexpected for me. I know now that they did this to keep me surprised, keep expectations to a minimum and go with the flow, otherwise I would try to influence it.

You see, although I see spirit and hear them, I am always skeptical to say the least, I want them to appear solid, have a cup of tea and give me their diaries to save me the trouble of trying to work out their lives. Now, although that has happened, minus the cup of tea, and it was amazing, it is just not often enough and that bugs me, but I am learning daily that they don't have to appear solid, they are there, you just have to believe in that fact and let it go.

The messages will come and they will let you know how they want to work with you in very subtle ways. You will suddenly find yourself intrigued and fascinated by the pyramids of Egypt, or find a deck of Tarot in a second-hand store and become enamored of them, or you will doodle and it will turn out to be an amazing portrait of your guide! Either way, they will let you know what they want to help you with, but it is up to you to believe in yourself and work with them, or tell them that you are not ready yet. The thing is, your guides only want to help you with things that you have already chosen to do before you came here and are just reminding you to get on with it. It's just sometimes you are just surprised at what it was you chose to do that you wonder why on earth you didn't figure out that you should go to art school!

I figured the answer to this one watching my husband doing some psychic art for the first time, he is an amazing artist, but because he knows about art, he tried to control it and that interferes with the process. Whereas I have no clue where I'm going with a piece of art, so they have a blank canvas to work with (in so many ways!) I don't try to control it because I am not sure where the next stroke will take me, but my husband already has the next ten strokes worked out in his beautiful artistic head.

Anyway, those portraits of the extraterrestrials were the beginning of me realizing that my art was recognized as someone real and that gave me confidence to do more, but then it stopped, zero, nothing came through. They were gone!

I wandered around the house, wondering why they had left and realized that in all of this I had let the house go to wreck and ruin and it needed an update. So out with a different kind of paintbrush, a scrubbing brush and a whole lot of willpower. Time to get the house in order. Which I suppose is a break of sorts, right? No, I know, but you have to make yourself believe there is a reason in all of this, right? When Spirit seem to disappear it is usually to make you get on with the routine tasks of life or to deal with some physical issue, that is all, and when it's done, they will be back to remind you of your spiritual work.

In the meantime, lights were going on, noises in the bedroom at night, doors closed and voices were heard, but nothing too crazy, just a reminder that they are there watching over me and waiting to carry on with our work.

## Chapter Four

## Go With The Flow

As soon as I had finished the decorating, the big jobs at least, the urge to draw came again. Partly, I think, to calm me down as there were so many things on my mind to do, and partly to teach me more as they began with some very awkward things like veils and feathers which again, I had no clue how to draw. But I trusted in their guidance and made an attempt, which is what they like, trying to do it, making an effort and showing them that you are seriously trying your best. It is only then that they will come and work with you. They need dedication and they have surely got that with me. I may not be the best psychic artist, but I am a trier and they love that. So no matter how bad you are at drawing, don't give up, they will come and help you more and more with time, all you have to do is give them that time.

So, I started drawing again and decided to do my son's guides and my husband's guides, well, you have to start somewhere and these guides were coming through.

Let me walk you through this one to show you what I mean about starting from scratch and how they help you. First of all, the feathers came, agh! I had no clue how to draw them, but I drew one and then copied it, (they are okay with this, no use using up hours of your day if you can reproduce it, it saves time and was not that important to the process. I had learned the basic feather and that was that.) They know how impatient I am, so I am sure they gave me a break on that one. The second thing was the hair, that was so hard. how on earth do you get a shine on hair and that was what I was hearing, 'My hair is very shiny!' I did the black, then tried with the white over and over but it just liked like white and black paint, and then I heard in my head, 'Make it fuzzy, increase the size of the brush.' I did this and there is was, a shine on her hair. I was thrilled to bits and moved on to the face. Agh! Drawing faces with nothing but a feeling and a quick glimpse of the spirit is daunting to say the least, but there are pointers along the way. 'Too big, too small, wider, shorter.' And so on, until you come up with something that feels right.

You find yourself drawing dots, as if in a dream, doodling and wonder what the hell you are doing that for, who on earth has dots on their forehead, but then it seems right and you carry on and when it is all over you understand why you had to do them.

You also find yourself doing intricate details, taking ages to draw a design or the little beads and you wonder why you are going to all that trouble and then you hear,' I used to love making beads' and you know why.

This guide was from the Inca people and loved her people very much. She was very artistic in her time and loved to create and show her people how to make things. When the art was done she asked that the hands were put in, to show my husband that she will help him with his psychic art and his paintings. My husband has since seen this guide whilst at a workshop.

This beautiful guide showed me more feathers, so I didn't really get away with it, but you can but try. I did not know how to draw a nose at this angle and this was the lesson in this drawing, they would not let me finish until I

got this right. I am happy with it. The hair, again, was a problem for me, but they worked with me until I could live with it. She has character and if full of life, a strong woman who didn't believe that only men could hunt, she was known for hunting along the men in her tribe and god help anyone who said she couldn't!

This beautiful lady came to as a guide for me and her name is Anne. It was time to learn about veils, beads and crosses. This one took ages, but it got there in the end. The thing is, they don't want it to be perfect, they understand how your mind works, and will make it a little harder and a little easier with each portrait, so keep at it, and it will get better.

And just to make sure I got the veil right, they gave me another one, and I'm sure there are much more to come. I'm getting there though. Now, the thing I want to tell you is this, when you are drawing with no knowledge, you are drawing blind. An artist who has trained knows the rules, how a garment flows and how the light shines on that garment. With no training you are in a sense blind to those things. So, what Spirit do is give me very clear, in your face, flashes of the garment, a curve on the shoulder or how it causes a shadow and then it becomes a little clearer. They are not necessarily moving my hand, although, in some of them, my hand moves quickly and bingo! The desired result is acquired, and at other times it is as if they slow my hand down and I have to draw in slow motion.

I was over the moon with these beads and I could almost hear them clapping from the other side. They are simple, but you have no idea how hard it is to get it right. I am not allowed to look up pictures of beads, I just have to listen or sense what they are saying and get on with it. I am tempted though, and I might if they come up with something like an aardvark or the like, I mean, come on!

This pretty gal came to me as my guide. Now how on earth do you draw teeth on a string! Again, easy, you draw one, get it as good as you can and then copy and paste. Like I said, they don't mind you doing this unless it is important to the overall message. For instance, say this was a person you once knew and she had a necklace that had one broken bead, then they would make you draw that extra broken bead. Here it was just to show that she too was creative and shows her status as princess of her tribe.

Her ears were the first ears to draw and to be honest I was ecstatic that they actually look like ears. I am glad she was happy with these, they are not that easy to do!

The other thing I would say here is this, if you are unsure where you are going, just doodle, color in the face, highlight something or fill in the background and let your mind wander as this will bring in more information from Spirit and even though you think you didn't hear anything, you suddenly have an urge to draw a necklace or a headpiece and you are back on track.

Again with the veils, but she was more interested in getting across her attitude to life, which was helping everyone, child, animal or enemy, it didn't matter to her, she just loved everyone and wanted to get that feeling across. I loved drawing this one as her energy just flowed all about me and I felt so serene and calm whilst in her company. That is the wonderful thing about psychic art, you get to meet the most wonderful people and they fill your world with such beautiful things, like loving energy and so much fun. They laugh, cry, feel sad or just dance around the room as I draw them, but each time there is so much love.

Like this beautiful lady, she brought the color red, passion and a feeling of letting go, and accepting all the love out there with open arms. They really made me work on the hair and how on earth do you draw folds in the dress, believe me, they work hard! But with each stroke you will feel you are getting stronger vibes from their world, messages pop into your head, a feeling, an idea and sense of what their lives were like. This woman was a dancer and loved nothing more than to dance around her people and bring passion and joy to their lives.

With each guide you will feel different, warm, cold, excited, happy, concerned, and so on. You might feel the need to paint in red first, as I did this one, and realize later on that the color red is very important in the message and all the meanings of the color red should be included in the message. Think about it, red, passion, warmth, love, excitement, and so on, all conveyed by just a color. Keep it simple, and you will understand by the end of the drawing that you have far more than you think you do.

The only mistake I did with this one is not draw in the gold jewelry that she wanted me to. It took me so long to get the dress and her hair reasonably right that I just hadn't got the energy to figure out how to draw gold jewelry, but I'm sure I'll learn in the not too distant future.

The gold was protection and a wonderful feeling of satisfaction and good fortune came with that, but luckily I was drawing for a woman who would understand.

When they want you to work on hair, boy do they go all out! This lovely guide is more of a feeling of the power of woman and all that entails. It's strange but the Magdalene is prominent with this energy, even though the hair is blonde, the energy is there. That is important when you are drawing people that you know cannot look a certain way, but want to show themselves differently, go with the flow, if the energy is there people will pick it up and they did with this one. Magdalene was recognized.

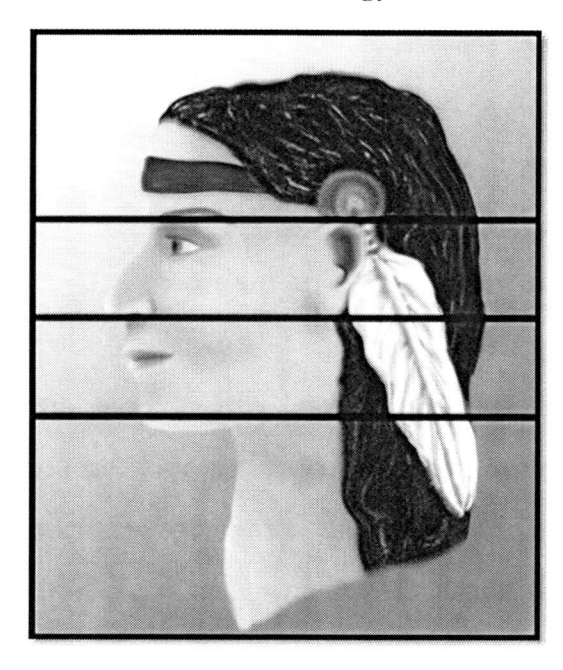

One thing I will say here to help you is that faces have proportions that are the same with every face and this will help you see if you are going in the right direction. It is a good base to start with and I only learned this after doing several portraits, but you can always go back and fix them, if you still have them nearby.

Here are the rules to help you get the face correct, and the nose not too long or the eyes too far apart. The ear is in line with the tip of the nose, and the eyebrow and the proportions are pretty much the same between eyebrow and end of nose and end of nose and chin in this one the chin is a little too long and the lips should be a bit higher, but all in all it's pretty accurate. Don't worry too much about this at first, but it all helps to make it as realistic as possible.

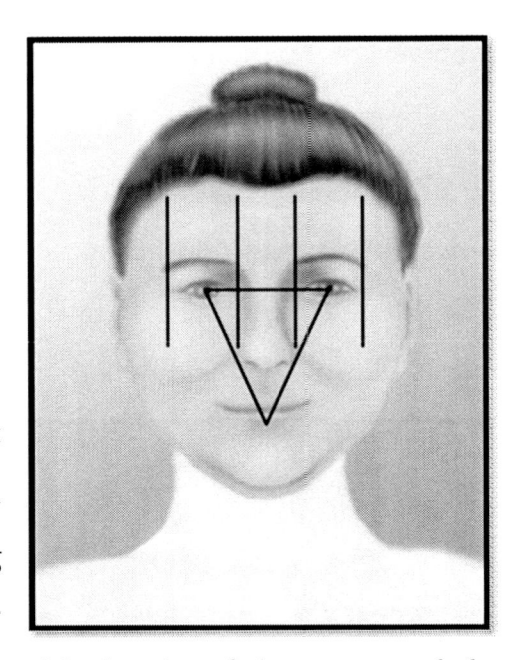

Here are some more diagrams to help you when you are drawing a frontal portrait and it really does make such a difference to your paintings. You see, even though Spirit help you with the drawings, they also want you to help them and if you try to get this right then this helps them a lot. They will not do all the work for you, after all, we are meant to be progressing together, so try to learn the basics for now and see how it will improve your drawings.

I this diagram you will see that distance between the eyes and the nose are the same, and there is an equilateral triangle flowing from the eyes, the edge of the nose and just below the lips. If you get these proportions right, then you will have a face that looks more real and then you can work on the personality of the person, like rosy cheeks, full lips or big eyes, but if you get the proportions right, then it will all look much better in the end. Some people draw Spirit with huge eyes out of proportion with the rest of their face and this is okay, but I found it hard to visualize the person in real life because of this, so I am trying to get it as real as a photo would be to give the client a better chance of recognizing their loved ones in Spirit.

This next diagram shows another triangle that helps you get the face right when doing a side portrait. The triangle points are the earlobe, the tip of the eyebrow and chin. Get this right and you are on the way to a very good drawing.

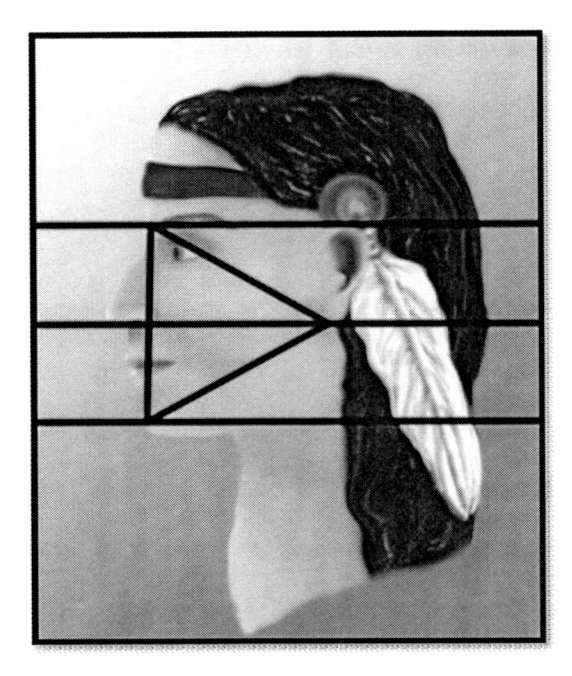

I think this is enough to learn to help you begin drawing your portraits and to help you see if they are life-like or not. When the times comes, there will be more to learn, I'm sure, but Spirit will guide you in this and let you know what they want from you. On the other hand, if you get this right they might just be happy with that and simplify the process so you can draw quicker and save some of your precious time.

In the beginning, it took me a day or more to finish a drawing, thank God the client wasn't sitting there waiting for me to finish or it never would have happened. That is why I like to do digital portraits, you can do it in your own time, change the color to suit, background, and hair color if you feel you should and so on. It saves me so much time. Imagine if I painted it and wanted to change the hair or the background, it would take ages, and I might even have to paint it all over again, so this gives Spirit more options.

## Chapter Five

## Be Happy With New Challenges

When they give you challenges and you are trying to make a living out of this as well as help people, be happy that the challenges are things that will make your hair turn grey. The harder the challenge the more you know they are working with you. Think about it, if you were faking it, would you give yourself hard things to draw? No, of course not, you would just draw the things you are comfortable with and leave it at that. But if you really want to work with Spirit they will challenge you to be the best you can, and like I said, you don't have to be brilliant, another Picasso or the like, but you do have to be open to being the best you can be and that is all they ask.

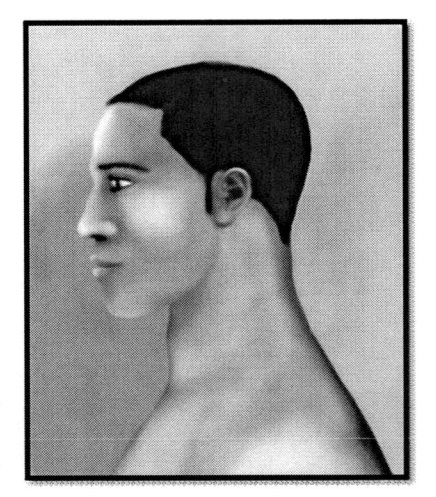

So here are a few of my harder challenges and you will see what I mean. One of the hardest things to do is draw someone you might know in Spirit and not try to manipulate it because of what you know. My son's twin is in Spirit and the urge was to draw him like my son, but the impression was that he was slightly different and so I did as best I could, and my son adores him. He knew about the differences by instinct and that wonderful bond twins have and so it confirmed for me that he was happy with it.

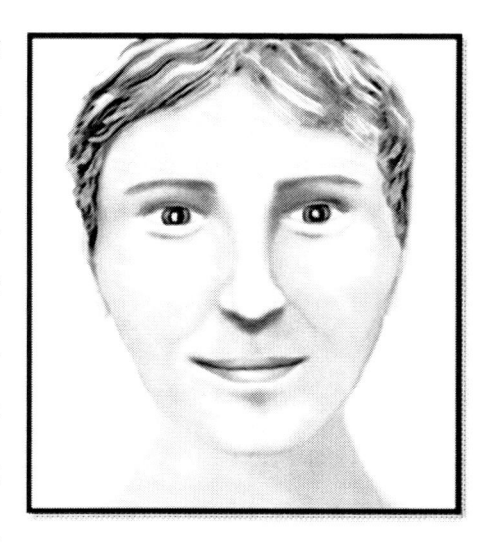

The other thing he challenged me with was the ear, he would not let me finish until I got it right. It's a first for me, so not too bad I'm thinking. But it doesn't matter in the end as long as they are happy with their portrait. That is all that matters. They have to be happy with it and even if the sitter doesn't like it, it is okay, the most important thing is that the spirit who came to sit for you likes it because then their energy will blend with it and it becomes something even more special than just a portrait. I have seen portraits smile, move and blink. I have seen them jump off the wall and their faces change, so believe me, when their spirit blends with the portrait you will have a little miracle on your wall that can change at any time. This one was hard to do and yet the easiest one in all. He is my brother in Spirit. The trouble is I have never seen him as he died before birth, so I have no clue what he looks like. In fact, I thought at first I was drawing a Native American Indian, I even did the black hair, but bit by bit I kept hearing, 'Not brown eyes, green eyes and not black hair, blonde hair' and so on, until I found I was looking at the face and something inside jumped for joy, I was suddenly very excited and happy and I heard, 'It's me, David!' and I hadn't really seen it until the end, but he looks like me! Strange how that happens, you don't really see the painting until the end and then it just jumps out at you, like this one did. They are very clever that way. If they don't want you to know what you are drawing, believe me, you won't until the very last stroke.

Now I know some of you are thinking, well that's easy, it's your own face, but you try to draw your face from memory, no mirror, or even with a mirror if you can't draw really. It is no easy task, and the thing that amazes me about this is that I have never seen David, he died at birth and yet, he managed to get me to draw the little details, like his lip curling up more on one side when he smiles, just like mine does. Another challenge, drawing someone that is older and plaits, beards and white hair. But to be honest, this guy led me through the process and it was quick. I wanted to finish it and fill it in a bit more but he said it was fine and was happy with it. I guess they just wanted to me to speed things up a little and be happy with it as it shows the essence of the person and that is sometimes all that is needed.

This guy was interesting. All I heard all day was, 'Crow!' and I was thinking, not on your Nelly! How on earth would I draw a crow! But I did and once again, they walked me through it, despite flapping about in a tizzy through some of it. Being patient with yourself is something I learned with this portrait, and once again, the crow is the important part of this portrait, so that was the part that they concentrated on the most. When I gave this guide to my friend, she had just had a very odd encounter with a crow the day before, so all in all, a very successful portrait. She now knows that that is one way in which he will let her know that he is around.

They made me work hard on this one, feathers were so important as was the young look on his face. His name turns out to be Little Chief, due to his youth. A beautiful soul that made me so happy to work with him. And I was thrilled to bits with the feathers! I was thrilled to have this accepted by a wonderful medium, who knew she had three Native American Indian guides working with her, but although she knew two of them, she was at a loss to know the third one. He showed up as a gift for her birthday and she was delighted. It amazed me as I did not know her birthday was near.

Like I said, go with the challenges and you will amaze yourself when you are finished. The harder the challenge the better you will become in the long run. So keep at it and remember that the challenges might be the most important part of the message, as in the crow.

The other challenge is to let all pre-conceived ideas go and just paint. Even if you don't believe in aliens, goblins, fairies, elves and so on, just draw them, they people they are for will understand in time why they are receiving such portraits. Just because you might not believe in them, your sitter might not only believe in them, but see them regularly, so be open and go with the flow.

You just never know what people will accept as their guide and for that matter, you will never know what people expect to see as their guide, or know as their guide. It might be a tree, an angel, a fairy or an extraterrestrial, but if you don't let your expectations go you will never know the range of guides they can show you. So if you find yourself drawing a tree and nothing else, let it happen and get the message that comes with it. Your sitter must then work out the meaning behind the tree, unless it came in the message.

The great thing about doing it digitally is that you can do whatever they want with the painting. For instance, this guide wanted me to draw it first, then color it is black and white and then change the colors to this. She wanted gold and blues in her painting and this is what she came up with. The person receiving her guide was delighted with it. Going with the flow and allowing them to influence your style allows them to convey messages and ideas that maybe you would not have picked up. This says more than maybe just a drawing would. She was affluent, powerful in her day and is still a very powerful guide in the Spirit world.

On the other hand you might get something like this! I kept hearing, 'Legions of Angels' and tried to draw

**Legions of Angels**

an angel, but it felt wrong, so I created an image that represents legions of angels. This piece was created for a good friend who does a lot of work for Spirit and I guess they wanted him to know that he has, not only one guide, but legions of angels working with him. I am sure they wanted to convey that they were not the kind of angels we think of, but extraterrestrials.

## Chapter Six

## Family in Spirit

When I got David through, my brother in Spirit, I had said the night before that it was wonderful to get guides coming through, but not many people know what they look like, so you couldn't really find out if this was exactly how they looked or not. I thought the only way I will know if they look like they are showing me is to draw family of people and see if I can match it up to photographs. I began to doubt that I could actually do that. I went to bed perplexed at the thought that maybe they didn't think I was good enough to move forward with this. The next morning, I noticed the light was on in my bedroom and that morning, David came through.

The odd thing about that portrait is that I thought I was drawing another guide, a Native American Indian, and somehow it morphed along the way into my brother. I only realized when I began drawing the eyes and seen there was something familiar about them and suddenly I heard, when the portrait was almost finished, 'It's me, David!' and I knew it was, not only from the portrait, but from the energy, he was so excited to get through and I realized that he was telling me that I could draw family.

The same thing happened with my son in Spirit, Mikey, I thought I was drawing a guide there too, but it morphed into Mikey and I only realized at the end of the portrait when I drew the neck, it reminded me of Joe's neck, his twin.

You see, that's the thing with Spirit, they are all someone's guides in a sense, Mikey watches over Joe and David watches over me, so although they are family, they are also guides. We all have a family member watching over us, just as we watch over family members here. We are all someone's guide and they are our guides, so in that sense, I was already drawing family. I know with my guide, I was in a past life with him, but in this life, he guides me.

I am learning to trust in their guidance and not to kick and scream all the way through the process. Obviously it will take time to get it right, and you have to be patient with yourself, but in the end, if you are dedicated enough, it will turn out okay in the end.

I am reminded about the footsteps in the sand quote, you know the one where there are only one set of footsteps and the person asks why God has left him and God says, I was carrying you. Well that's how it is with working with Spirit, you might think they are not there, but they are, you just have to believe in yourself and know that they are always willing to work with you. If it is not working as well as you expect it to it's because you just don't believe you can do it. You can, and if you stick with it, you will see the difference.

So, back to drawing family. I thought I would give it a shot and come up with a person for one of my friends on Facebook. I got a grandmother and luckily my friend knew who she was just from the message. The message said she was just like her and did the same things she did. My friend is very creative and loves to be outdoors, just as her grandmother did. So one down, several hundred to go. But it's a good start I thought. You see, it doesn't have to look exactly like the person in Spirit, it just has to have some features that let the sitter know that they are family, maybe a prominent nose or the same eyes or maybe even a pair of glasses that are unusual. For now, this will suffice to prove survival of Spirit.

The next portrait have not been owned and that, of course, brings you down a bit, but he came for another reason. Sometimes they have their own agenda that might not fit in with yours. The first one was a coach of some sort and kept saying he loved the 'Red Sox' baseball team. I thought it was maybe someone's grandfather, so I put it up. He looked very sad and no matter how hard I tried to make him smile, he just looked sad.

I didn't get much more information with him, except that he was a good coach and loved sport of any kind. So I decided to look up where the 'Red Sox' were from in America and realized it was Boston. Then I knew why he was so sad. The disaster at the Boston Marathon had just occurred and he was showing his sadness that this could happen.

The next one was an eye-opener to say the least. It was a child, a very quiet child, I couldn't get a word out of her. But such love and light with her that it was an absolute pleasure to draw her. Then when it was finished, I thought, this reminds of me of another psychic artist and how she used to draw, Coral Polge, and then, (duh!) I remembered a message I had in church many years ago that Coral wanted to work with me. I had laughed at the time because I had no intention of drawing Spirit, but I felt she influenced this drawing and it felt good. This was the first one that felt so relaxed and easy to do, well, it just sort of happened on its own, without too much huffing and puffing from me. No one had owned her yet, but I honestly think she popped in to remind me about Coral. So you see, they have their agenda and are always helping you, you just have to be open to what they are saying.

This journey is turning out to be more exciting than I

thought. The light goes on and off now like clockwork and I know it's their way of saying I'm on the right track. I just love Spirit, they are way ahead of us, if only we could trust enough and believe in ourselves we could do so much more.

The next guy was very odd, he started off as a dapper, ladies' man, from Victorian times it seemed, monocle, rich clothes and he told me that he was very handsome, but then, he turned into a priest! I understood from the look in his eyes that something happened that he felt he needed to do penance for, possibly a girl dying from an abortion, something he was very ashamed of and so he decided to join the priesthood. He made a very good priest, but the shame of causing something like that remained.

The drawing itself was wonderful to do and so quick now. The hair first, that's all I saw, shining, shimmering hair, then I heard the eyebrows are bushy and when doing the eyes he said he wanted the eyelashes pointing down, which seemed crazy to me, but it worked!

I think the moustache is from his dapper days and not really suited to priesthood I feel. The other thing that I found odd were the eyes, I drew them as looking straight ahead, but as by the time the painting was finished, they were looking down. They never cease to amaze me.

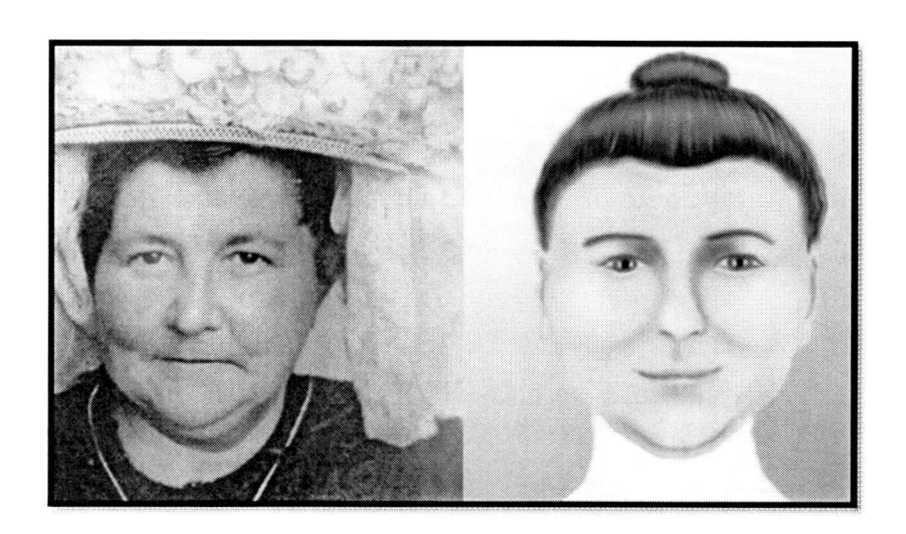

I will show you some more family portraits and some photos to go with them. Here is a photo of a grandmother who taught me a big lesson – listen to the guidance and stop trying to control it, even if it seems wrong, like black hair in a grandmother, it is not for me to decide what I think is right, but go with the flow and listen to the person coming for the sitting. I began this painting and I knew straight away it was an older woman, so I began drawing white hair, but she kept saying, 'Darker, darker!' and I didn't listen and when I drew her face it was very round, so I made it a little thinner and she said, 'No! Keep it round!' and of course, I didn't listen, but it felt wrong when I made it thinner. Anyway, I gave it to my husband and he said, exactly those two things, her face was rounder and her hair was dark.

I nearly gave up there and then, I felt that I was useless at painting and was angry at myself for not listening, but the day I decided to give up, she came back and said, 'Give it another try.' So I did and this is what I got, then and only then did I look at a photo my husband gave me of his grandmother and was astonished. It's not exactly like her, but it was a good attempt and there are bits of it that tell you it's her, like her chin, the bit of hair that hangs down in the middle, her eyes and her rosy cheeks.

I also got the name Maria with this and rosary beads. Her second name is Maria, which I did not know and she always had a pair of rosary beads with her. So not bad for the first few portraits of family. Like I said, I nearly gave up as I am the most impatient person on the planet, but like she said, 'Give it another try!' If you do this, and keep the portrait of the sitter for a while before you give it, then you can go back and work on it to get it right. When it is right, you will feel it.

## Chapter Seven

## Step by Step

In this chapter I will show you how the process works with me and what they say, or the feelings I get and what I see to help me finish the portrait. In this portrait I saw the Spirit standing behind me. I didn't get the feeling that she was anyone's family, just helping me with this chapter, which was very kind of her. The overall feeling with her and what she showed me was her hair. It was long and flowing over my shoulder, so I began with this. I did one side and then copied it and pasted it to the other side. That's a start, then I filled in around her neck with hair..

Next came her face, there is no guidance here, you just feel your way around the picture for now, the rest will come as you do your best to fill in the space. You might get the eye color or just be drawn to a color for now.

You can draw one eye and copy and paste the second for now, you can fill in details later on. This is just to use as a guide for now. Next you can tidy it up a bit, as this takes no concentration and while you are doing something relaxing, you can receive more guidance, like highlights and such, which I fill in a bit here and there to come back to later. She is coming along, her face was not in the middle, so I moved that to line up with her hair. This felt right for now. Next you can give her a proper neck and chin, she let me know that she needed something else, the shoulders were wrong and the hair needed fixing, but that's okay, that will come.

I tidied up her hair as much as I could and it felt right, but her face still looked a bit gaunt and pale, so I asked her if she was happy with it and the feeling I got was to add more color and fix her up a bit more, so I did. I also got the feeling that there was still something wrong with her hair, but wasn't sure what yet. I knew if she would not let me finish it until it was exactly right for her, so I didn't mind and carried on adding color to her face and neck. She looked a whole lot better in the next layer, so I thought I was finished, but not so, there were a couple more things to do.

I thought she meant just crop the picture and that was that, but she wanted more done and she let me know by a feeling in the pit of my stomach that said it was not quite right. I kept looking at her hair and feeling that something and she wanted me to change it, but wasn't sure yet. Also, I got the feeling that she wanted clothes, so I had a cup of coffee and waited a few minutes to see what came to me and I saw the clothes so I ran upstairs to the office and began her dress, nothing elaborate, just something to show she was wearing a dress. She was happy with that too. Then it came to me, she had chestnut brown hair and that was all she wanted to show, so I darkened it a bit and I heard, 'That's it!'

Her name is Roseanna and she is a lovely soul who just wanted to help me show you how the layers are built up and how they inspire you every step of the way.

Okay, I'll show you one more and this one was a doozy when it came to the hair. Like I said, it starts off one way and you just never know where it is going to lead, that is what I love about psychic art, it's amazing how they take you on a new journey with each piece.

It started off with a curl, that was it, just a curl, and then I saw a little girl with curls. So I did a mess of curls to see where that would lead.

I heard, 'My hair is smaller and I have blue eyes', so I worked on that next and waited for something else to come. She told me her name was, Rebecca and she was full of giggles.

I just could not get her hair to turn out right, something

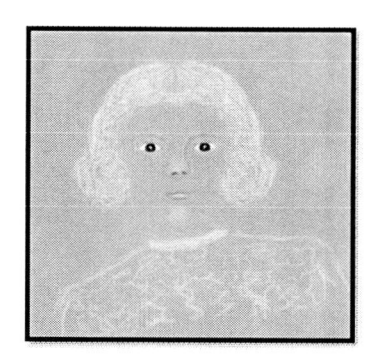

didn't feel right, but I waited and knew that it would come, so in the meantime I worked on her nose and lowered her eyebrows a little. Then it came to me, she had ringlets! I added the ringlets and it felt right, then I worked a bit on her nose again, her chin and her neck. The better it got, the stronger she became and I could see her smiling, so I fixed her lips a little, added her clothes and tidied her up, she was very happy with the result. But I can tell you, it was no easy job to sketch this little girl. Sometimes it's easy, sometimes you have to work hard at it and listen very carefully to Spirit but I know they always guide me in the right direction in the end. I'm very happy with this one, and here she is, Rebecca.

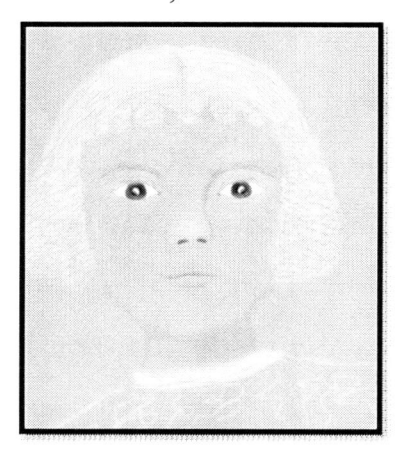

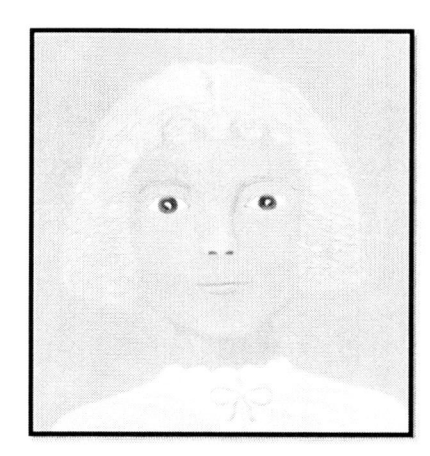

## Chapter Eight

## Messages

Now with all portraits there will come a message of some sort for the sitter. Do not worry if this is not coming straight away, as it can be hard for you to pick things up when you are practicing your psychic art. Let the art come first and then wait, the messages will come in some form or shape.

Just understand that they have it covered and that even if you do get names, places and such things, the sitter might not have known the person coming through, they might be a great aunt, or a great-grandparent who just wants to come and say hello. In these cases, the only thing you have is that there might be a family resemblance and that might be enough for the sitter to place them.

Like I said, for now, don't worry about the messages, or you will stop it instantly. It is hard to still your mind when you are learning a new skill. The best thing I found is to just get on with the drawing and begin talking to the spirit who has come. They may answer straight away, or they might wait until the portrait is finished, either way, they will want to give you the message, so if it is not coming whilst doing the portrait, give it time, sit with the finished painting and see what comes afterwards, you will be surprised at how much you will receive.

The other important thing to remember is that when you are drawing, the physical symptoms of a headache or the like may well be the Spirit trying to show you how they suffered or even how they passed to the world of Spirit, so always be sure at the end of a session to cleanse the energy and release the symptoms as they do not belong to you. The wonderful thing about this is that you can feel the person, a loving feeling, or agitated, sad or happy, their personality will come through and this alone can be a wonderful message for their loved ones here. Feel them, let them draw close to you and you will find that the messages become clearer in time.

There is nothing to be afraid of when contacting Spirit, put a circle of light around you and the people in Spirit who come through, that was you are protected from other energies and can focus on the Spirit who is there. Sometimes you might get one of two Spirits coming together and that might be confusing, so be sure to tell them what you want and how you want to work so your guide can regulate the sittings with Spirit. You don't want a room full of Spirit all jumping in at the same time otherwise your portraits would be a mess. Be in control of your gift and ask your guide to allow them in one by one, this will help if they are all rushing in together.

Some of the portraits you do will not be recognized or will not have a photo as people didn't have cameras like we do today. So a lot of families didn't have family portraits, especially if they were poor. Don't let this put you off and keep asking Spirit to send people that can be recognized and they will come in time.

## Chapter Nine

## Drawing Your Guide

I found that drawing my own guide was a nightmare. First of all you have all kinds of ideas of what he looks like in Spirit and though you may catch glimpses of him, or even turn into him as I did once (he overshadowed me to the point where I was him for a few minutes), it is still hard to draw your own guide if you know them.

I tried several times and I felt it was wrong, something just wasn't right, and that is a good indication that they are not happy either. When you start to draw your guide, just let it go, don't hand on to expectations, just let them guide your hand, as this is a wonderful opportunity to work one to one with your guide.

Here is my guide, I had to draw him several times to get the one that he was happy with and thankfully, I 'm happy with it too. I like his hint of a smile, as he is always having fun with me and this is so appropriate. Not only did he come through for me, but he also helped with the eyes and I honestly think these are the best eyes so far.

Well, I hoped your enjoyed my journey into the world of digital psychic art, and I hope that you gain the confidence, as I did eventually, to draw to for people and bring the gift of a portrait from their loved ones. It really is the most amazing gift from Spirit and it will be so appreciated by Spirit and the people who ask you to draw a portrait.

Practice on family and friends to get going and don't let anything stop you if you want to do this professionally. Spirit don't mind that you ask money for your portraits, money means nothing to them and they know that you have to earn a living and use your time to do these portraits. The bills are still going to come, so don't worry about asking to be paid for your services. It is like any other job, except your boss is you. Spirit don't tell you what to do, they guide you, but you are the boss and decide when and how much time you want to spend working for Spirit. But if you are like me, you will spend all your spare time building up a rapport with Spirit and the wonderful people who come through.

Of course you will have people say you are making this up, or you shouldn't charge for this and several other things that are negative, but don't worry, that is only their opinion and it does not affect you in any way, so ignore the negativity and carry on. Remember, Spirit love what you are doing and the people you get the portraits for love that you are sharing your gift with them, so enjoy it and carry on doing what you feel is right and you can't go far wrong.

One last thing, give it time, don't rush yourself and enjoy every minute of it. Spirit love to work with us and have the patience of saints, so there is no need to feel down if you don't get it right the first, or even the hundredth time, they will give you all the time in the world to perfect your gift of psychic art.

Another thing that I thought would be good to tell you is that animals can come through from the world of Spirit and even if you have never painted one, give it a try, you might be surprised at the results. Here are a couple that came through for my sitters.

These were my first and the dog was actually black in life, but scruffy with a happy little face and that is how the sitter recognized him. So it does not have to be perfect yet, if they want to find something to be recognized by they will and sometimes, the painting might not be for the sitter, it may be for their neighbor or friend and they have not seen it yet. Believe me, if Spirit come through, it is for someone to recognize them and in time, the people who are meant to see the portraits will see them. Like this dolphin, I wasn't sure why I was drawing it, but I had just done a guide drawing for a client and this little guy popped in, so I knew it was a special gift to her to go with the drawing of her guide. He told her that he would be in her dreams of the ocean and was a guide. She wrote back that she had seen him in her dreams and that she knew he was her animal totem and even had another artist draw him for her. So you see, just go with the flow and it will all turn out okay in the end.

I doubted my ability several million times during this journey, but then I see the look on people's faces when I give them a guide and hear how happy they are and it makes me realize that to not use this psychic avenue would be sad.

One other thing I would like to share with you is this, you can draw people, spirit people and even people alive, as sometimes they need healing and Spirit will encourage you to draw them to give the family of that person the heads up on their condition, but you can also draw animals and scenes like this one. I got this when I asked my guide if I should proceed and this is what he showed me, a scene from his past, a loved one about to bear his child, his dog, horse and his home, everything he loved. It was as if he was showing me that these are the things that endure, loved ones and companions along the way and that they can still communicate through this wonderful medium.

The wonderful thing about digital art is that you Spirit have much more leeway and can change and add things along the way, especially if you have other art, as I do, to add to the wonder of the portrait. Here is another picture to show you what I mean.

You can add symbols and scenes to fit the feeling of the guide and save yourself a lot of time and effort is you have already done a painting of a scene that you would like to see in your portrait. Spirit don't mind what you do, they are more interested in getting the portrait to the client and adding what you feel is right is good for you on all levels as it helps you to open up to Spirit, as does all creative pursuits in the realms of art.

I did a painting for a client and the guide who came through was helping me in so many ways that I did not even realize it until the painting was finished.

When I sent the painting the client, she said that she was not sure if this was the one she had seen in a dream, as he was young in the portrait and her guide was much older. I did another couple of guides with this one, but her guide kept coming back, so I decided to draw him again and see what happened, this time he was a bit older and still, she was not sure if this was the guide she saw in the dream. I then told her that no matter how hard I tried to paint him differently he keeps showing himself as he is in the portrait. Then, it all changed, she told me who her guide was and it turns out that he is a famous guide of a well-known medium, 'White Eagle' and when I put the only painting of the guides together, guess what, it was him!

I ended up doing three portraits of him, not looking at the previous ones and still he looks similar. I will show you here how I had to show the guide to convince this lady that it was the same guide. I took the headdress of the famous guide in the painting and put it on the guide I had drawn and showed her and only then did she decide that this was her guide. Of course, my painting is not as good as the original painting, but this is all 'White Eagle' had to go on to get me to paint the portrait. The thing to remember is this, most people forget what their guide look like, even in dreams, or they have a particular idea of what their guide should look like, but that is not necessarily so, let the guide help you draw him and you will find that somewhere in between the portraits, if you do more than one for practice, then you will have the real guide that wants to show himself as he really is, or as close as you can get. After all, remember, it takes time to tune in and find the right understanding of how Spirit work with you. I learned that when I am trying to draw a line, say on his forehead and I am not getting it right, then it is wrong and eventually I will figure out that he had no lines in the photo he is working from.

You see that is how they work, from old photos of themselves that they had taken while alive so that they can help you confirm it is them. They may even have a favorite photo that they want reproduced as such and so they will work with you until you get the light right and the face in the position of the photo. When you are first drawing, this can be difficult, as I found out when this guide said draw me a bit to the side, which was hard for me, but then I eventually gave in and stop trying to control it and did as I was asked. That is the problem sometimes, we limit ourselves in our thinking, when really we should just trust in their help to get the work done. This guide showed me that he was helping me but that I had not completely let control go and it would have been a much better portrait if I had. Here he is wanting to look spectacular in his gorgeous headdress for my client..

In the end, it took me several portraits and I learned a lot from doing them, so don't be afraid to draw several in the beginning, it all helps to make you a better instrument for spirit and if the client is happy, and of course the guide, then that is all that matters.

Just remember this, spirit do not have faces or bodies anymore, they are working in the dark just as much as you are in that sense, so they have to focus on an old painting or try to project how they looked to you through your senses. How amazing is that! This is what you have to remember, how amazing it is, and even if you only get the nose right, or the eyes in the first sessions, keep on keeping on because in time it will improve and Spirit have all the time in the world and are the most patient of all teachers.

And if you think you are not succeeding because you did not get the whole face correct to the last line, then like I said before, try to draw your face from memory without a mirror and you will see how wonderful Spirit truly are when it comes to guiding you. Be happy with each little result and remember to thank them for teaching, guiding and smiling when you throw the pens in the air and say you are done! Then pick up your pens and say thank you again as you grow in Spirit and learn that they love it every time you reach deep inside and find the strength to carry on.

Since these early portraits the faces have become more detailed and the fight to give this up has faded into the background when I get a good vibe with the faces I am drawing for Spirit. I will show you some of the latest ones that I did for practice, asking spirit to help me with details and I do hope you can see the difference in my art in just a few short weeks. Please, give it a try as it will be so rewarding for you and will give a great boost to your sitters.

I do hope this helps you in some way and puts you on the path of the most wonderful medium of psychic art, as there is nothing better than showing someone the face of their loveds in Spirit.

Love and light

Saleire

Saleire's Website: www.saleire.com